Powerful Prophetic Prayers
to Speak Over Your
Children.

By: Cisum Mai

ISBN: 979-8-9867008-5-4

DEDICATION

This book is dedicated to the Glory and Honor of my Lord and Savior Jesus Christ who abundantly supply all my needs according to His glorious riches.

This book is dedicated to all the wonderful gifts and blessings that have been presented to us as parents, grandparents, aunts, uncles, & leaders from Heaven above, our beloved children.

This book is dedicated to all parents, grandparents, aunts, uncles, and leaders who desires to speak words of life into and over your beloved children, grandchildren, nieces, and nephews

CONTENTS

1 INTRODUCTION

In these days and times like no other days and times the words spoken over our beloved children matter more than we will ever know. The magnitude, love, power, comfort, and life, that comes from the words we as parents, grandparents, aunts, & uncles speak truly have a life changing effect. The power rest within our words. The words spoken into and over our children determines whether the life changing effects experienced are positive. Our children are such great watchers and imitators.

They watch with great attention every move and every word. Has there ever been a time where adulting was taking place and you were so caught up in the moment of being an adult, that when you took a stepped back from what you were engaged in all eyes were on you? Soaking up your every move, every word, and every detail. I am sure that has happened to a vast majority of us over our parental journey. I know for sure it has happened to me more times than I would like to even mention. One specific time I recall so vividly, I was on a business call speaking to a gentleman about a product that I had ordered. The order was incorrect, it appeared the product was no longer in stock, so rather than refund the out- of-stock item they decided to send what they had instead of what

I ordered. After having a very nice discussion with the gentleman at the store he was able to resolve the issue over the phone without any extra delays. It worked out perfectly even better than expected. After disconnecting the call my son Excellent Jamal looks at me and said, "Dad even though the wrong item came that worked out awesome, and the guy was very nice, that was an awesome way to handle that call dad." I replied to him, "Oh wow thank you very much my champion son!" Inside I was completely shocked. I had no idea he was paying attention to how I was handling the conversation, what I was saying, how I was saying it, consuming it all. What I saw taking place was a young man engaged in building his Lego universe and having fun playing with his action figures. While engaged playing he's simultaneously watching and hearing everything that's going on. Our children are some amazingly clever human beings. They are so very special and truly brilliant. We must stop thinking that our children are too young to comprehend or understand things. We must also give them credit for their amazing intellect. As consistent examples for their viewing pleasure; we are studied closer than close. We are the ones our children try to imitate first. Although it is all well and great to have children imitate their parents, we as parents should be great pointers and point them to our Lord Jesus Christ. The most perfect example. As we keep our eyes on Jesus Christ, looking to Him for all our needs, His word declares "I will instruct you and teach you in the way you should go; I will counsel you with my eye upon you." (Psalm 32:8 ESV) He will supply us with every good and perfect gift. "Every good and perfect gift is from above..." (James 1:17 NIV). To some children their dads are SuperHero's; to some their moms are SuperSHEro's; to some their grandparents have GrandPower; to some their aunts are Besties; to some their uncles are FUNcle's. What a special way to be seen by our children. As we receive revelations, understanding the magnitude of this power we can strategically, and continuously speak words of life and greatness over our children every day. We can speak in their presence, while they are resting peacefully, while they are away at school, or even while they are outside playing. At any point or time during the day or night, quite time, meditation time, or walking through nature time. Powerful prophetic prayers can be spoken over and into the lives of our beloved champion children. Our words have so much POWER they can cause death or give life. "Death and life are in the power of the tongue…" (Proverbs 18:21 KJV). It is our choice as to what we will choose to speak over and into the lives of our beloved champion children every day of their richly blessed, highly favored, deeply loved, and prosperous lives.

2 YOUR WORDS MATTER

Why do our words matter when it comes to our children? Children look to parents, grandparents, aunts, uncles, and leaders for reassurance, confirmation, validation, that stamp of approval. Your words carry a lot of weight, value, and truth. Plainly stated our words **MATTER**! We must really understand how much weight and validation our words carry with our children. How often have you found yourself being asked a question by your beloved child, niece, or nephew such as: How does this look? What do you think about this?

What should I do? Where should I go? When the time for big decisions or major moves come up whose input is most often requested? Parents, grandparents, aunts, and uncles. Your words really matter. That is why it is so very important that we speak words of life and life more abundantly over our children. Some may say I don't speak bad over my children. I don't curse my children or speak death to them. Yes, I totally thought the same thing until I was shown a powerful revelation in the book of Mark 11:14. This verse talks about when Jesus and His disciples were leaving Bethany, Jesus was hungry and saw a fig tree in the distance, He went to reach for fig and found none. Then he said to the tree, "May no one ever eat fruit from you again." Now, as we look at the statement

Jesus just made towards the fig tree, this statement is a curse. Jesus cursed the fig tree. Jesus didn't yell. Jesus didn't use any vulgarities. Jesus didn't even raise His voice, yet the words Jesus spoke were a curse that killed the fig tree to its roots. Now let's think about that in relation to some of the statements spoken into and over our children. The statement m a d e by Jesus was a simple statement saying, "no man eat fruit from this fig tree forever". Which is like saying to our children, "You always late! You don't ever get it! You are working on my nerves! You are so clueless! These are just a few statements spoken and heard over time. Never would I have thought speaking like this at one time, and hearing these statements being spoken would be considered speaking curses into and over lives of my children. It is truly a matter of death or life regarding our spoken words and weight these words carry in and over the lives of our children. There maybe someone who has not had contact with their children in some time. Some may feel as if their children will not allow them to pray for and over them since they are much older now. My middle son Jamree Jamal is 26 years young and no matter his age or his location on the planet, I will always speak these powerful prophetic prayers over his life, be it in his presence or in his absence. He is always my beloved champion son in whom I am always well pleased. Even as parents our Lord Jesus Christ calls us sons and daughters "And I will be a Father to you, and you shall be sons and daughters to Me," says the Lord Almighty

(2 Corinth 6:18 AMP). We are all His beloved children. Our Heavenly Father is always gracious and welcomes us with open arms. As with our children they are never too old and there is no distance that is too far to speak these powerful prophetic prayers in and over their lives. It is never too late to start speaking and declaring with the double anointing king and queen priest power that is given to us as believers. "But you are a chosen people, a royal priesthood, a holy nation, God's special possession…" (1 Peter 2:9 AMP). This power has been given to us as believers in our Lord Jesus Christ. It is totally up to us as parents, grandparents, aunts, uncles, leaders, and figures of authority in the lives of our children to speak these powerful prayers over their lives so that

they are always covered, protected, and prosperous with the mighty and powerful word of the Most High Living God.

3 SPEAK LIFE

It is such a powerful privilege for parents to always speak life into and over our children, more now than ever before! We must watch our words diligently because words have such great power. Words have the power to wound or to bless, and when we speak without care or negatively it will cause damage to those we are speaking to as well as ourselves. Think of it this way, we are the only created beings with the ability to verbalize, this privilege was only given to us who was created in the likeness and image of God. As we come to realize the power and magnitude of our words as well as the power and magnitude of this ability, we have which is to speak, we will always fair better when we consult the Lord Jesus Christ in how to respond or how to best use our powerful words concerning our children. We as parents, king and queen priest over our children can ask the Holy Spirit to help us before we respond or reply to any situation or experience concerning our children. With the help of the Holy Spirit, we can be assured we are always speaking life as well as words that encourage and build them up. There is great power in our words. It is our words that will settle everything when it comes to our beloved children, and it is so very imperative and important that we speak these powerful prophetic prayers over and into our children every day! The age and location of our children does not matter, the only thing that matters is that we as king and queen priest speak these words with faith and allow our Lord and Savior Jesus Christ to do what HE does best and that is bless, prosper, protect, supply, comfort, heal and love us unconditionally. His word declares, "And my God will liberally supply (fill until full) your every need according to His riches in glory by Christ Jesus" (Philippians 4:19 AMP). Listed below are some powerful prophetic prayers you can began to speak over your beloved children daily! The power is in our **SPOKEN WORDS** and the **RESULTS** are in **JESUS PERFECT HANDS** in JESUS MIGHTY NAME AMAN!

Powerful Prophetic Prayers:

1. You are a true gift from heaven above!
2. You are the Best Son or Daughter!
3. God's favor is all over you!
4. You have the favor of God with your friends, teachers, and mates.
5. Divine protection is over you!
6. You are redeemed!
7. You are a blessing going everywhere to happen!
8. You are the apple of God eyes!
9. When God looks at you, HE sees you righteous!
10. You can do all things with God on your side!
11. God Delights over you with singing!
12. God always causes you to be at the right place at the right time to be a great success!
13. You are highly favored!

14. You are richly blessed!

15. You are deeply loved!

16. When I look at you, I see the glory of the Lord Jesus Christ!

17. As Jesus is so are you in this world!

18. The Lord Jesus Christ will cause you to prosper in all things!

19. You bring so much glory to the kingdom of God!

20. You are destined for greatness in Christ Jesus!

21. You are more than a conquer!

22. You are a beloved champion son or daughter of God!

23. You have a powerful mind, with great ideas!

24. You will do great and mighty exploits for God Kingdom!

25. You are God's Masterpiece!

26. God is always well pleased with you!

27. You are God's chosen one!

28. Treasures of life flows out of you!

29. You are a beacon of light shining bright for God's Kingdom!

30. You are unique just like your fingerprint!

31. You are the sun the brightens the day!

32. You always make great choices and decision!

33. The Lord blesses you and be gracious to you!

34. The Lord prospers you in all things!

35. You are a born winner because the Lord is with you!

36. I see the love of God in you!

37. You are mighty in the Lord Jesus Christ!

38. You are very successful!

39. God hands are all over your life!

40. You walk in the Spirit because you are led by the Spirit!

41. You are blessed with the wisdom of God!

42. You have the mind of Christ Jesus!

43. You have the heart of Christ Jesus!

44. You walk in God's divine favor!

45. Rivers of living water pour from you!

46. Everything you do prospers for your great and God's glory!

47. You are a beautiful branch connected to the living vine!

48. You bring forth great fruit in every season of your life!

49. You are blessed among all people on earth!

50. You have an amazing destiny!

ABOUT THE AUTHOR

Cisum Mai... pronounced (Sis - Sum - My) is a
beloved child and disciple of The Most High GOD.
He is a beloved son, brother, uncle, father,
instrumental music composer for (TV Sync, Movies,
Internet Videos, TV Commercials, Network TV,
Video Games, Independent Films, etc.) as well as
an author. Cisum Mai appreciates having the
opportunity to share his instrumental music with
the planet as well as sharing the GREAT NEWS
known as the GOSPEL OF JESUS CHRIST with all that
he is blessed to encounter. There is no greater joy
in this world than leading precious souls to their
wonderful and loving Savior JESUS CHRIST!
Whenever there is a chance or opportunity to
share the LIFE changing word of JESUS CHRIST with
anyone that will listen it is truly a game changer for
both the sharer and the receiver! Be Blessed,
Enriched, Favored, and Protected in the Name of
Our LORD JESUS CHRIST! AMEN AMAN AMEN!

Made in the USA
Columbia, SC
14 March 2024